Modern Etudes for

Low Clarinets

James Marshall

WWW.MELBAY.COM

Preface

I wrote this book for students and colleagues to satisfy the need for low clarinet material to use as studies and in competitions. While it has become commonplace to use soprano clarinet material for low clarinets, there is the inherent problem of their ideal tessituras or ranges not being the same. The fact is soprano clarinet etudes were never intended for use by low or bass clarinets.

Many students contribute to the sonority of their school bands by learning the bass clarinet. Most schools' own instruments that are standard equipment to be passed on from year to year, student to student. Experts in the field know that these instruments can't play higher than G5, yet many state competitions require the low clarinets to play soprano clarinet etudes that go a full octave higher.

The pieces in this book are primarily for low clarinet, but their contemporary nature makes them appealing to soprano clarinetists in the rich chalumeau to moderate clarion registers. Instead of encountering notes that are too high, however, soprano clarinetists will occasionally find notes that are too low; for example, in the instance of the low E-flat of the bass clarinet that occurs in some of these studies, soprano clarinetists will need to transpose these notes up by an appropriate interval.

Modern Etudes for Low Clarinets utilizes modern motifs, frequent meter changes and rhythms that are idiomatic to the low instruments. Nine of the etudes are original and four pay homage to Bartok, Hindemith, Debussy —after *La cathedral engloutie* (The Sunken Cathedral), and Stravinsky—*The Rite of Spring.*

James Marshall

Contents

Etude No. 1
Adagio Sostenuto

James Marshall

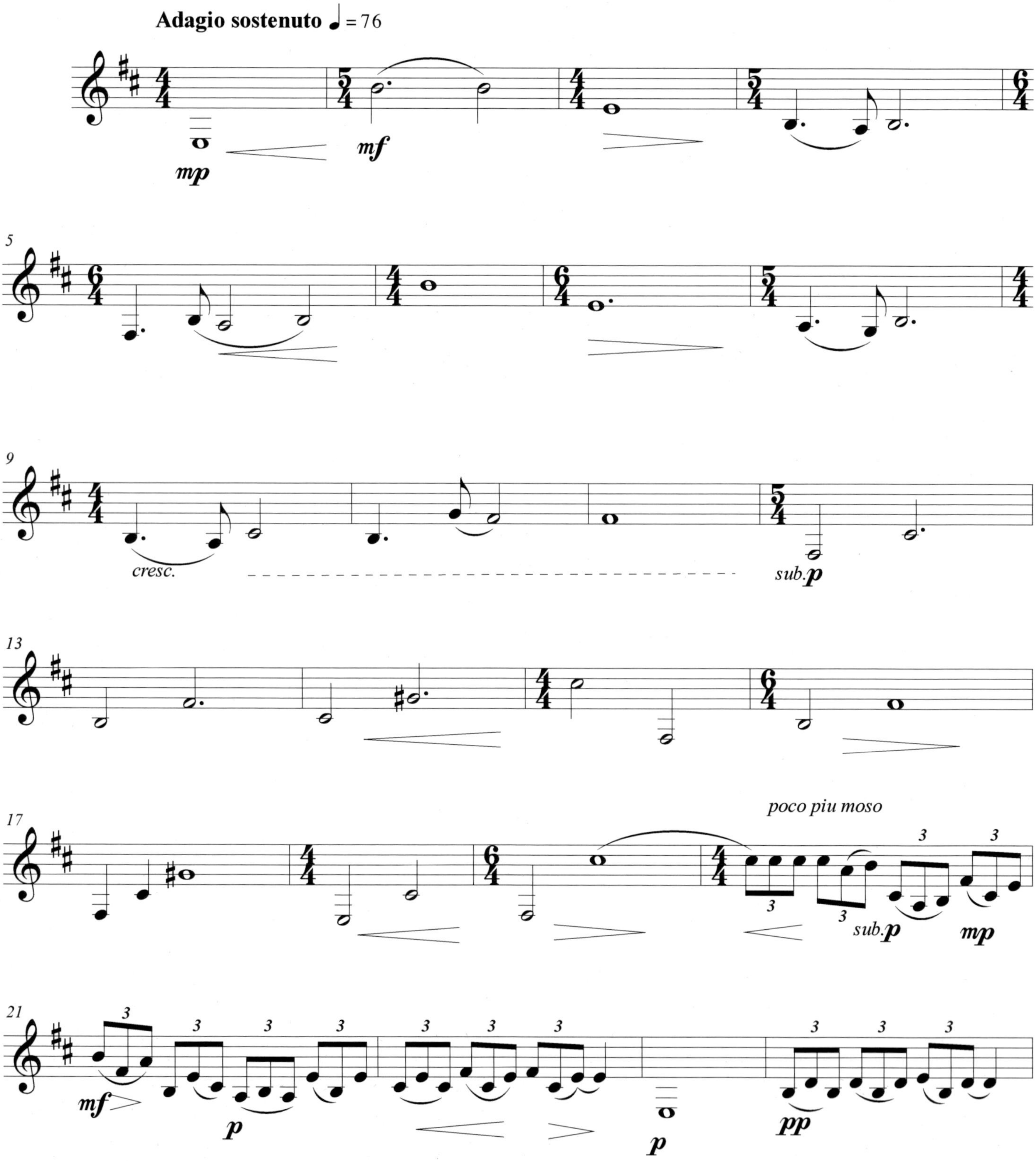

Adagio sostenuto ♩ = 76

mp *mf*

cresc. *sub.* ***p***

poco piu moso

sub. ***p*** *mp* *mf* *p* *p* *pp*

sub.p
cresc.

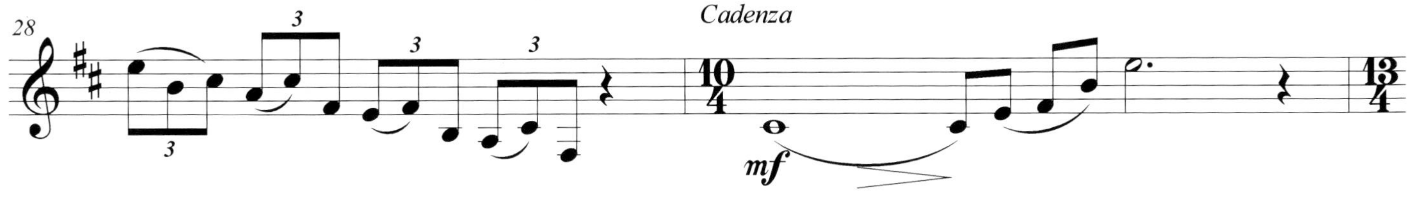
Cadenza

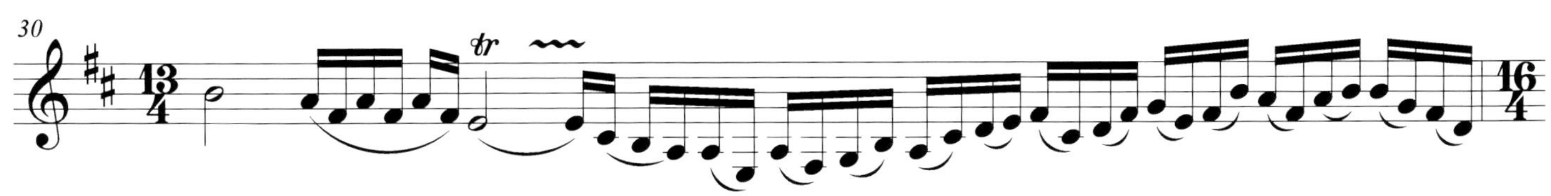

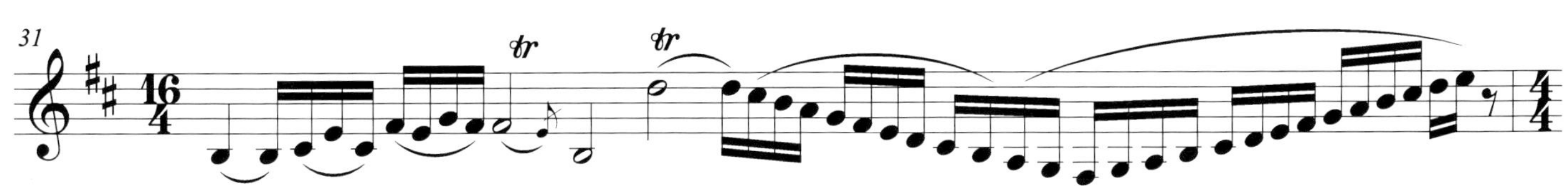

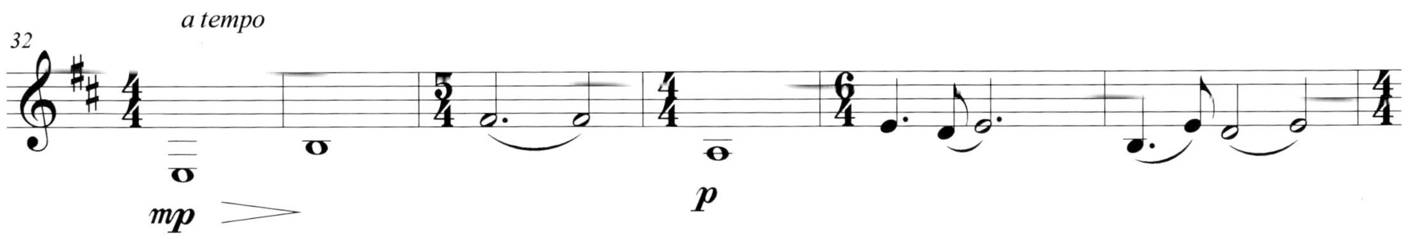
a tempo

dim.

Etude No. 2
Andante con moto

James Marshall

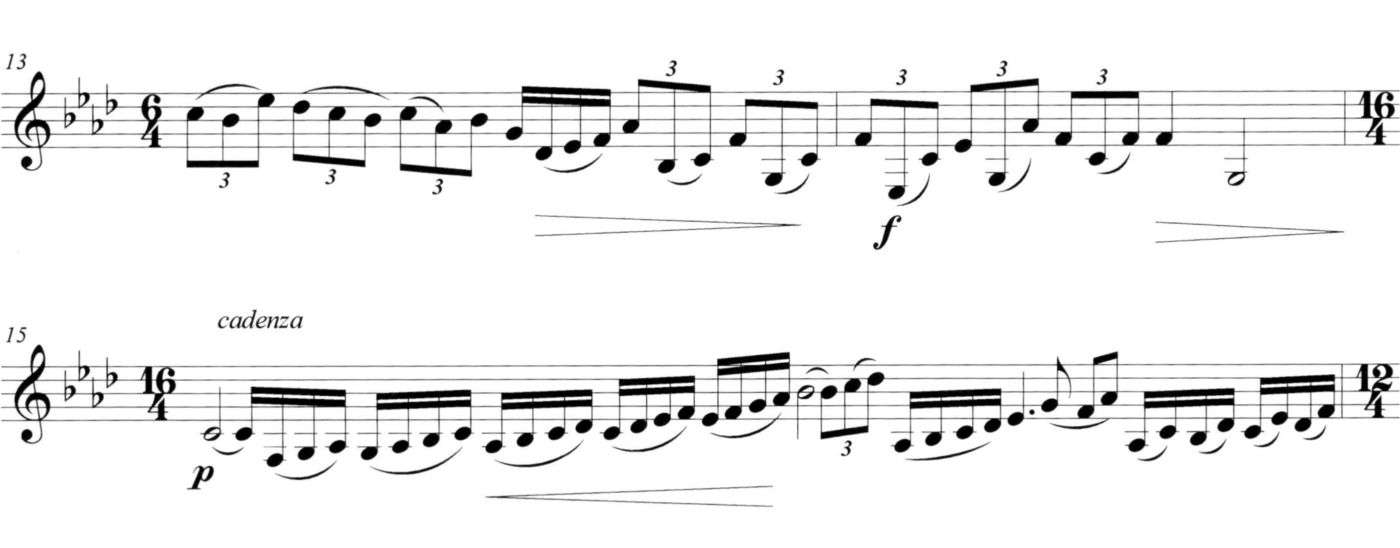

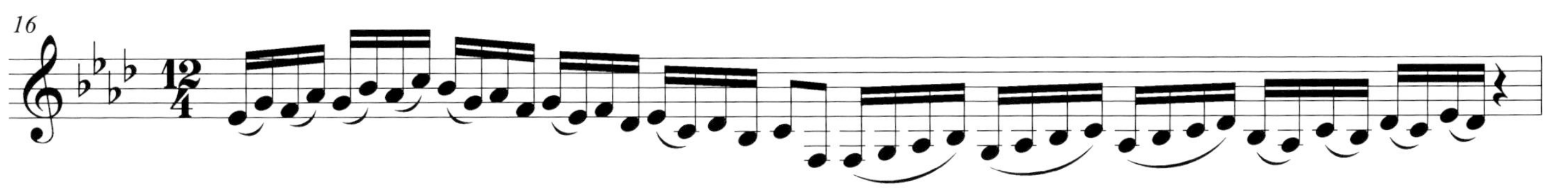

Presto

Etude No. 3
Allegro giocoso

James Marshall

Etude No. 4
Allegretto

James Marshall

Etude No. 5
Allegro Moderato

James Marshall

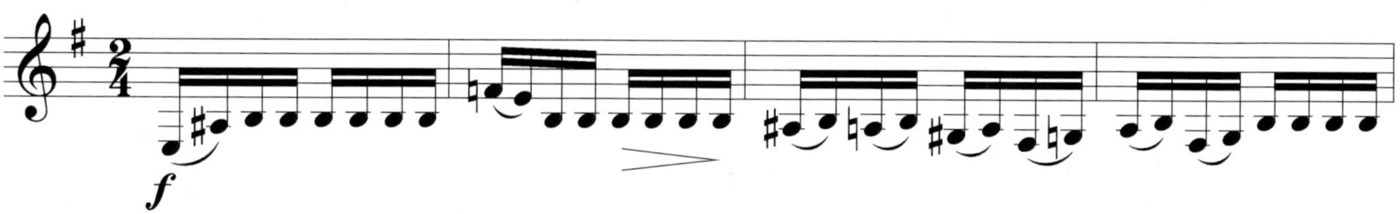

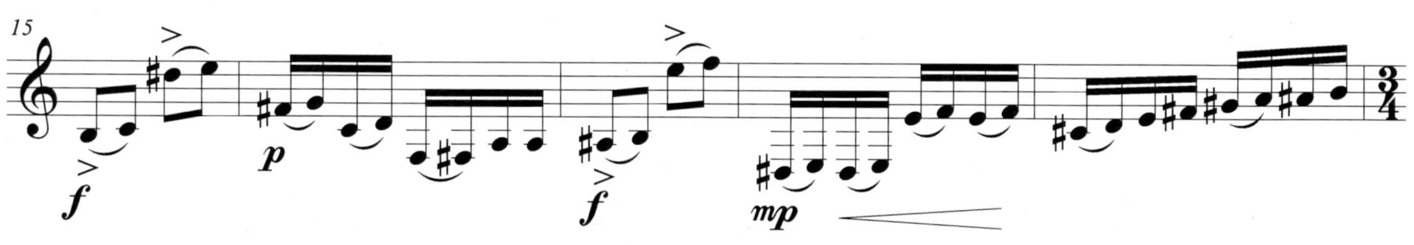

23
p
cresc.
tr
tr
tr

28
tr
mf
tr
mp

33
mf

37
f

41

Etude No. 6
Allegro guisto

Bass Clarinet

James Marshall

This page has been left blank to avoid an awkward page turn.

Etude No. 7
Allegro

Bass Clarinet

James Marshall

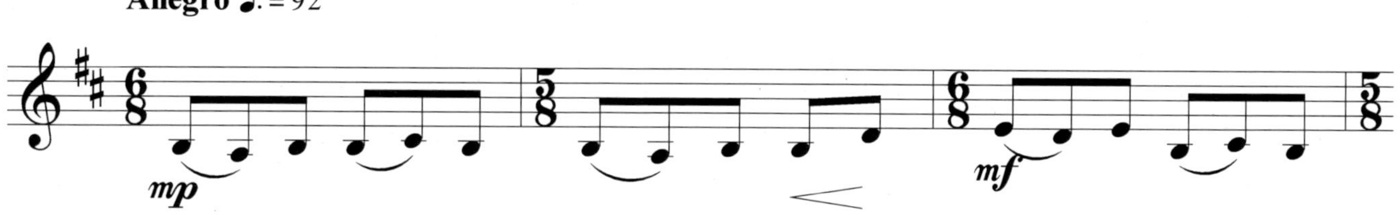

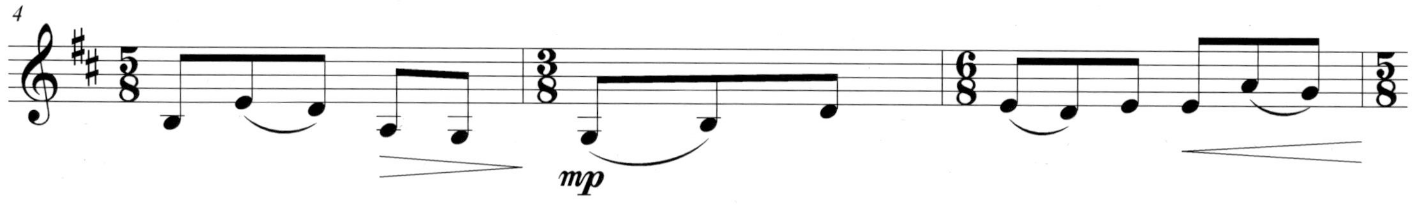

subito p
p
mf
mf
mp

Etude No. 8
Lento con moto

Bass Clarinet

James Marshall

This page has been left blank to avoid an awkward page turn.

Etude No. 9

Adagio - Allegro con fuco

Bass Clarinet

James Marshall

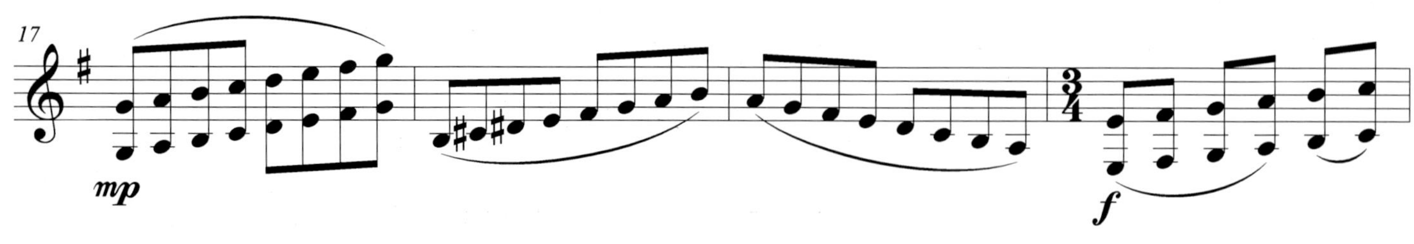

21
mf
25
cresc.
f
29
mf
mp
33
37
mf
41
mp
mf
45
f

Etude No. 10
Homage to Paul Hindemith

James Marshall

Homage to Paul Hindemith - Langsam ♩ = 66

mp

Ziemlich schnell ♩ = 102

mf

f

mp

mf

p

dim.

pp

p

This page has been left blank to avoid an awkward page turn.

Etude No. 11

Homage to Bela Bartok

James Marshall

Homage to Bela Bartok - Sostenuto appassionato ♩ = 62

p *mf*

3

mf

Vivace ♩ = 132

5

pp *cresc.*

9

rall.

mf *p*

13

Tempo I

mp

accel.

♩ = 106-116

Allegro giocoso

15

sempre staccato

mf

19

23

p

27
31
♩= 92
35
p
38
poco piu mosso
cresc.
42
f
sempre staccato
46
rit.
Presto ♩= 144
pp
49
52
Tempo I
Presto ♩= 144
f
mp
f

Etude No. 12
Homage to Claude Debussy

James Marshall

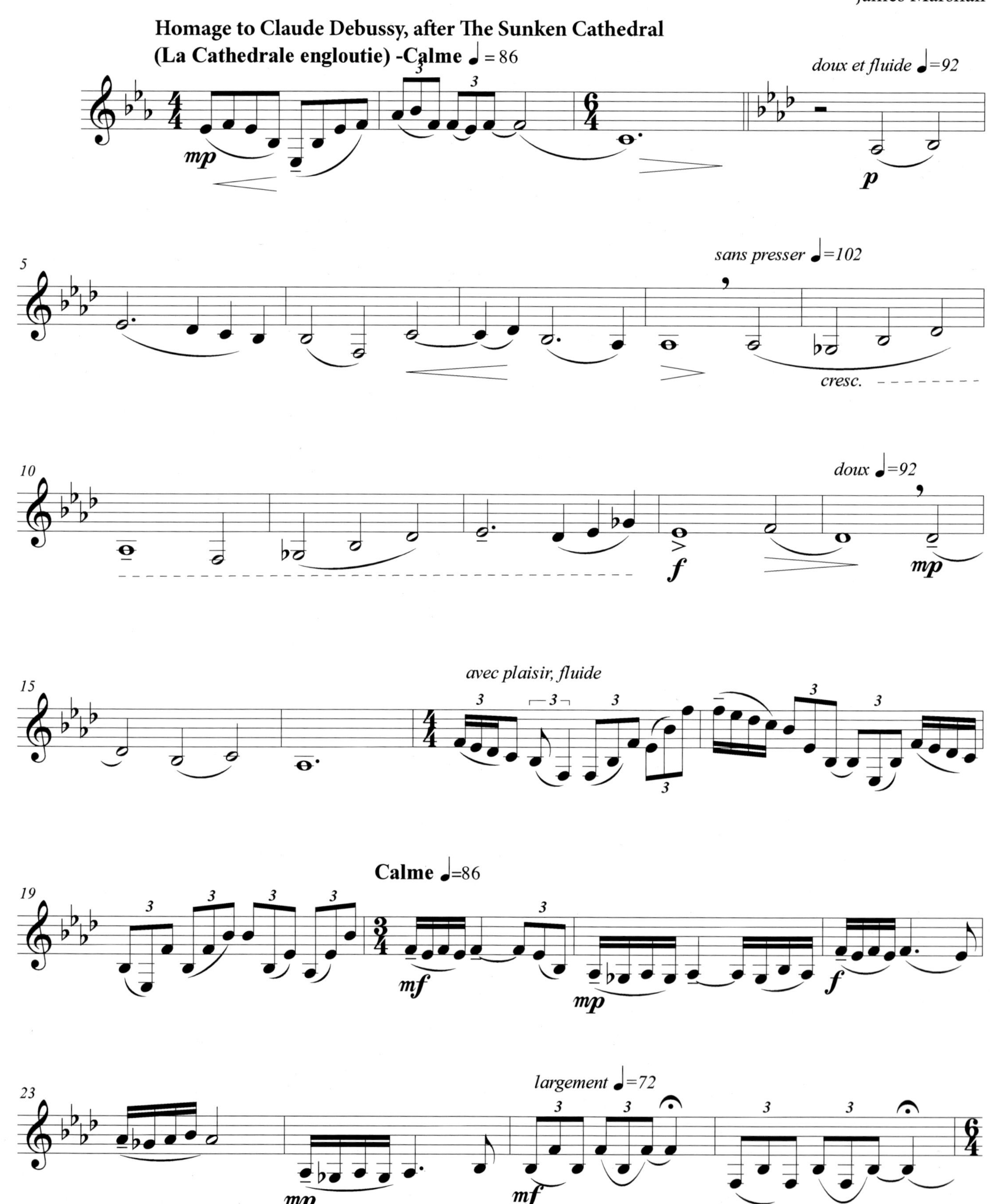

doux et fluide ♩=92
presser
ralentir
Profondement calme, largement ♩=80
presser
lentement ♩=76
cresc.

Etude No. 13
Homage to Igor Stravinsky

James Marshall

Homage to Igor Stravinsky - after The Rite of Spring
Le Sacre du Printemps Lento ♩ = 50

tempo rubato

p *mp*

4

Tranquillo ♩=108

8

p

12

pp *p*

16

mp *dim.*

20

Allegro rhythmico ♩=100

f *p*

27

f

34
mf
42
mp
52
p
mp
59
mf
cresc.
Presto ♩=116
f
65
mf
f
ff
70
mf
f
p
75
mf
80
Maestoso ♩=66
5
5
ff

Other Mel Bay Clarinet Books

101 Easy Songs for Clarinet (Maroni)

Beginning Clarinetist's Songbook (Maroni)

Easy Classics for Clarinet with Piano Accompaniment (Spitzer)

Easy Duets for Clarinet (Puscoiu)

Fun with the Clarinet (W. Bay)

More Fun with the Clarinet (W. Bay)

Solo Pieces for the Beginning Clarinetist (Heim)

Clarinet Solos on Balkan Folk Songs and Dances (Puscoiu)

Easy Klezmer Tunes (Phillips)

Klezmer Book (Galper)

20 Clarinet Duets from Baroque to the 20th Century (Heim)

25 Solos for Clarinet from the Unaccompanied Works of J. S. Bach (Leonard)

Baroque Music for Clarinet (Heim)

Classical Repertoire for Clarinet Volume 1 (Puscoiu)

Favorite Student Clarinet Classics (W. Bay)

International and Classic Favorites for Clarinet Solo (Heim)

Laurindo Almeida: Duets for Clarinet and Guitar

Mozart for Clarinet (Heim)

Music of Brahms for Clarinet (Heim)

Recital Pieces for Clarinet from the Period of Impressionism (Heim)

Solo Pieces for the Beginning Clarinetist (Heim)

Solo Pieces for the Intermediate Clarinetist (Heim)

Solo Pieces for the Advanced Clarinetist (Heim)

Christmas Solos for Beginning Clarinet Level 1 (Heim)

Instrumental Caroling Book (W. Bay)

My Very Best Christmas: Trumpet, Clarinet, Soprano Sax & Tenor Sax (Khanagov)

Sacred Melodies for Clarinet Solo (Heim)